BALL PYTHON MASTERY

Essential Care, Breeding, and Health Tips for Enthusiasts

Nii Yeboah

Table of Contents

INTRODUCTION

Ball pythons are one of the most popular and fascinating pet reptiles, known for their docile nature, striking appearance, and relatively easy care requirements. Whether you're a seasoned reptile enthusiast or a beginner, understanding how to properly care for and breed ball pythons is essential to ensuring they thrive in captivity. This guide will take you through the basics of ball python care, from setting up the perfect habitat to understanding their unique breeding behavior. In this complete guide, we'll explore everything you need to know about raising a healthy ball python and successfully breeding them. You'll learn about their natural habitat, ideal tank setups, feeding routines, and how to maintain a proper environment for them. When it comes to breeding, we'll cover everything from selecting the right pair to providing the right conditions and understanding the complex reproductive behaviors of these beautiful creatures. By the end of this guide, you will have the knowledge and confidence to take on the exciting challenge of caring for and breeding ball pythons, all while ensuring their health, happiness, and well-being. Whether you're in it for the joy of keeping a pet or looking to start your own breeding program, this guide is here to help you every step of the way.

WELCOME TO THE WORLD OF BALL PYTHONS

Ball pythons, scientifically known as Python regius, are one of the most beloved pet reptiles due to their gentle temperament, manageable size, and striking beauty. Native to the grasslands and forests of West and Central Africa, these snakes are often found in the wild coiled up in tight spaces, hence the name "ball python" – a reference to their tendency to curl into a ball when they feel threatened.

Known for their stunning array of color morphs and patterns, ball pythons are not only captivating to look at, but they are also relatively easy to care for, making them ideal for both first-time snake owners and experienced breeders. They are non-venomous constrictors, using their strength to subdue their prey rather than venom, and they typically grow to a manageable size of 3 to 5 feet, making them a perfect pet for those with limited space.

As you venture into the world of ball pythons, you'll be amazed by their calm and curious nature, which makes them perfect companions for those looking for a low-maintenance reptile. Whether you're here to learn how to properly care for one or to dive into the exciting world of ball python breeding, you're about to embark on a fascinating journey into the care, behavior, and reproduction of one of the most unique creatures on Earth.

PURPOSE OF THIS GUIDE

The purpose of this guide is to provide a comprehensive and accessible resource for anyone interested in ball pythons, whether you're a first-time owner, an experienced breeder, or simply fascinated by these incredible reptiles. Ball pythons are a fantastic choice for reptile enthusiasts due to their manageable size, calm temperament, and stunning variety of color morphs. However, their care and breeding require a solid understanding of their natural behaviors, habitat needs, and health requirements.

This guide is designed to walk you through the essential aspects of ball python care, including creating the perfect environment, feeding practices, health management, and understanding their behavior. We'll also dive into the intricacies of breeding ball pythons, from selecting healthy breeding pairs to managing the delicate process of egg incubation.

By the end of this guide, you will have all the information you need to ensure that your ball python thrives in its environment and, if desired, breed successfully. Whether your goal is to care for a single pet or embark on a breeding venture, this guide will serve as your go-to resource, offering expert advice and tips to help you navigate the world of ball pythons with confidence.

WHO THIS BOOK IS FOR

This guide is tailored for a broad spectrum of readers, from those considering their first ball python to experienced breeders looking to deepen their knowledge and refine their breeding practices. If you are a first-time reptile owner, this book will introduce you to the fundamental aspects of caring for a ball python, ensuring you create an environment where your pet can thrive. It is also ideal for reptile enthusiasts who want to expand their understanding of ball pythons' biology, behavior, and breeding. For experienced breeders or those interested in entering the world of ball python breeding, this guide offers in-depth insights into the nuances of genetic traits, morphs, and the breeding process. You'll gain a thorough understanding of how to select healthy breeding pairs, optimize conditions for reproduction, and increase the likelihood of successful hatchings. This resource will also assist in navigating the challenges breeders face, such as genetics management and the optimal incubation environment. In addition, this book is for hobbyists interested in the unique genetic variations of ball pythons. The diverse range of morphs available today requires an understanding of both the genetics involved and the ethical considerations of breeding for specific traits. Whether your goal is to care for a pet or pursue ball python breeding professionally, this guide will equip you with the expertise needed to ensure your success.

As with all fields of reptile care and breeding, knowledge is continually evolving. This guide presents the most current best practices while encouraging further learning and adaptation to new developments in reptile husbandry.

CHAPTER ONE

UNDERSTANDING BALL PYTHONS

What Are Ball Pythons?

Ball pythons (Python regius) are non-venomous constrictor snakes known for their docile temperament, manageable size, and distinct behavior of curling into a ball when threatened, which is how they got their name. Native to West and Central Africa, these snakes typically grow between 3 to 5 feet in length, making them one of the smaller species of pythons. They are named for their unique defensive posture of coiling tightly into a ball, which offers them protection from predators in the wild. Ball pythons are primarily nocturnal, spending their days hiding in burrows or under rocks, and are carnivorous, feeding on small mammals, birds, and occasionally amphibians. They are constrictors, meaning they subdue their prey by wrapping around it and squeezing until it suffocates before swallowing it whole. In captivity, ball pythons are popular for their ease of care, friendly demeanor, and the wide variety of morphs (genetically inherited color and pattern variations) that have been developed by breeders over the years.

HISTORY AND ORIGINS OF BALL PYTHONS

Ball pythons are native to sub-Saharan Africa, where they are found in grasslands, savannas, and forests. They are particularly abundant in countries like Ghana, Togo, and Nigeria. In the wild, they tend to inhabit burrows or crevices in the earth, seeking shelter from the hot African sun. The species has adapted to these environments, developing a body structure that allows them to coil tightly into a ball when they feel threatened or stressed, offering protection from predators.

The ball python was first discovered in the wild by Western scientists in the 18th century, but it wasn't until the late 20th century that they became widely known in the pet industry. They were initially exported to the United States and Europe as exotic pets in the 1980s, with their popularity rapidly increasing over the years. Since then, they have become one of the most common pet snakes due to their calm nature, ease of care, and relatively small size compared to other pythons.

POPULARITY AND APPEAL IN THE PET INDUSTRY

The popularity of ball pythons in the pet industry has soared in recent decades. Their calm and docile nature makes them an attractive option for first-time reptile owners, while their manageable size (compared to other large snakes like Burmese pythons) makes them suitable for people with limited space.

Ball pythons also stand out because of the incredible variety of color morphs and patterns that breeders have developed over the years. From albino and piebald morphs to the more exotic combinations like pastel and clown, there is a ball python for every taste. This genetic diversity has made them highly desirable for reptile collectors and hobbyists, further fueling their demand in the pet market. In addition to their visual appeal, ball pythons are relatively low-maintenance, requiring only a proper enclosure, consistent temperature and humidity levels, and a diet of appropriately sized rodents. This ease of care, combined with their fascinating behavior and long lifespan (typically 20 to 30 years in captivity), has cemented their place as one of the most beloved pet reptiles.

COMMON MYTHS AND MISCONCEPTIONS

While ball pythons are widely considered one of the easiest snakes to care for, there are still many myths and misconceptions surrounding them. Let's debunk some of the most common ones:

1. "Ball Pythons are Dangerous to Humans"

This is one of the most common misconceptions. Ball pythons are non-venomous and generally very calm, making them an ideal choice for snake lovers. They are not aggressive and will typically only bite in self-defense when provoked. Even then, their bites are generally harmless.

2. "Ball Pythons Require Large Cages"

Unlike other large snake species, ball pythons do not require vast enclosures. In fact, they prefer smaller spaces where they can feel secure and hide. A properly sized enclosure with adequate hiding spots is essential to their well-being.

3. "Ball Pythons Don't Need Heat or Humidity"

Another myth is that ball pythons can thrive in any environment. In reality, they require a specific range of temperatures and humidity levels to remain healthy. A temperature gradient, with a warm basking area and cooler side, is crucial, as is maintaining humidity levels between 50-60%, with a slight increase during shedding.

4. "Ball Pythons Are Hard to Breed"

Ball pythons are relatively easy to breed compared to other species, making them a popular choice among reptile breeders. With the right conditions, including proper pairing, temperature regulation, and a suitable breeding cycle, ball pythons can successfully mate and produce healthy clutches of eggs.

5. "Ball Pythons Are High Maintenance"

While all pets require care and attention, ball pythons are among the more low-maintenance reptiles. Their feeding requirements are simple (they eat rodents, which can be easily obtained), and they are relatively low-energy, needing only occasional handling and basic environmental upkeep. Understanding the true nature of ball pythons is key to ensuring they live healthy and happy lives, whether as pets or as part of a breeding program. Dispelling common myths and focusing on their true needs and behaviors will set you up for success as you venture into the world of ball python care and breeding.

PREPARING FOR YOUR BALL PYTHON

Choosing the Right Ball Python for You

When selecting a ball python, it's important to consider factors such as your experience level, space, and what you're looking for in a pet. Ball pythons come in a variety of morphs (color and pattern variations), each with its own price range and care needs, so take your time to research which one suits your preferences. For first-time snake owners, it's generally recommended to choose a more standard morph, like a wild-type or pastel ball python, as these tend to be more readily available and are less expensive compared to rarer morphs. Wild-type ball pythons have the typical black and brown coloration and pattern, making them the most common type. Consider the size and age of the snake as well. Juvenile ball pythons are often smaller and more affordable but can be a bit more delicate, requiring extra care during their early development. Adult ball pythons are easier to manage in terms of feeding and handling, but they also require a larger enclosure. If you're specifically interested in breeding, understanding genetics is crucial. Ball pythons have an incredibly diverse array of morphs, and pairing the right morphs can help you achieve the desired traits in offspring.

SELECTING A HEALTHY BALL PYTHON

When buying a ball python, especially from breeders or pet stores, always ensure you're selecting a healthy snake. Here are some key indicators to look for:

1. Active and Alert

A healthy ball python should be alert and responsive when handled. If the snake is lethargic, unresponsive, or constantly hiding, this could be a sign of illness or stress.

2. Clear Eyes

The eyes of a healthy ball python should be bright and clear, without any cloudiness or discharge. Cloudy eyes can be a sign of a health issue, such as an infection or dehydration.

3. Clean Skin

The skin should be smooth and free from any wounds, bumps, or abnormalities. Ball pythons shed their skin regularly, so they should have an even, healthy appearance. Rough or patchy skin can indicate malnutrition or a skin infection.

4. Healthy Weight

Gently feel the ball python to assess its weight. The snake should not be too thin or excessively obese. A well-fed snake will have a slight layer of muscle and fat, but it should not have visible bones sticking out or be overly bloated.

5. No Signs of Parasites

Check for visible signs of external parasites such as mites, which may appear as tiny dark spots on the skin. Internal parasites may cause lethargy, weight loss, or regurgitation, so it's important to keep an eye out for any signs of illness.

If possible, request to see the snake's feeding history and health records before purchasing. A reputable breeder or pet store should be transparent and offer you this information.

COMMON HEALTH ISSUES TO WATCH FOR

Though ball pythons are generally hardy creatures, they can still face health issues. Here are some common concerns and how to spot them:

1. Respiratory Infections

Symptoms: Wheezing, mouth breathing, nasal discharge, and open-mouth breathing.

Cause: Poor humidity levels, improper temperatures, or unsanitary living conditions.

Treatment: Seek veterinary care immediately, as respiratory infections can be fatal if untreated. It's essential to address any underlying environmental issues to prevent recurrence.

2. Mites and Parasites

Symptoms: Visible small black specks (mites), loss of appetite, excessive scratching, or skin shedding problems.

Cause: Mites can be introduced from other reptiles or unclean enclosures.

Treatment: Mites can be treated with reptile-safe mite sprays, and your snake may need a vet-administered treatment for internal parasites.

3. Obesity

Symptoms: A bloated appearance, sluggish movement, and difficulty moving.

Cause: Overfeeding, especially with large prey items or too frequent feedings.

Treatment: Adjust feeding schedules and monitor portion sizes. If obesity is severe, consult a vet.

4. Shedding Problems (Dysecdysis)

Symptoms: Incomplete or problematic sheds, often with retained shed around the eyes or tail.

Cause: Low humidity or poor hydration.

Treatment: Increase humidity, soak the snake in warm water, and provide appropriate shedding surfaces.

5. Internal Parasites

Symptoms: Lethargy, weight loss, abnormal feces, or regurgitation.

Cause: Contaminated food or exposure to infected environments.

Treatment: A vet may prescribe deworming treatments or antibiotics, depending on the type of parasite.

Regular vet checkups and proper husbandry practices can help minimize the risk of these common health problems.

HOUSING REQUIREMENTS FOR BALL PYTHONS

Providing the right habitat is essential to keeping your ball python healthy and happy. Here's what you'll need to consider when setting up an enclosure:

1. Size of the Enclosure

A 40-gallon tank or similar-sized enclosure is ideal for adult ball pythons, but a smaller 20-gallon tank is sufficient for younger snakes. Ball pythons are not highly active, so they prefer a secure, confined space that mimics their natural environment.

2. Substrate

Choose a substrate that is easy to clean and provides a comfortable environment for your snake. Popular options include aspen bedding, coconut husk, or cypress mulch. Avoid using sand or gravel, as these can cause respiratory issues or ingestion problems if swallowed.

3. Hiding Spots

Ball pythons are shy creatures and will feel more secure with access to hiding spots. Provide at least two hiding places—one on the warm side and one on the cool side—so your snake can retreat when it feels stressed.

4. Water Dish

A clean water dish large enough for your ball python to soak in is necessary. It should be changed regularly to prevent contamination and provide hydration.

5. Climbing and Enrichment

While ball pythons are not natural climbers, providing branches or logs can add enrichment to their environment, allowing them to explore their enclosure and feel more at home.

TEMPERATURE AND HUMIDITY GUIDELINES

Ball pythons are native to warm, humid environments, so maintaining the right temperature and humidity in their enclosure is crucial for their health.

1. Temperature

Ball pythons require a temperature gradient in their enclosure, with a warm basking area and a cooler area to regulate their body temperature.

Warm side: 88–92°F (31–33°C)

Cool side: 75–80°F (24–27°C)

Use a heat lamp or heat mat on one side of the tank to provide the necessary warmth, but always monitor temperatures using a reliable thermometer. Avoid using heat rocks, as these can burn your snake.

2. Humidity

Ball pythons thrive in moderate humidity levels.

Ideal humidity: 50–60%

During shedding, increase humidity to around 60–70% to aid in the shedding process. You can maintain humidity by misting the enclosure or using a humidity gauge to monitor the levels.

3. Nighttime Temperatures

Ball pythons don't require a drop in temperature at night, but the temperature should not fall below 72°F (22°C). If your home tends to get cold at night, consider using a ceramic heat emitter that doesn't emit light but still provides warmth.

Proper temperature and humidity management are key to keeping your ball python healthy, as improper conditions can lead to shedding problems, respiratory infections, and stress. By preparing your ball python's habitat with the right size, temperature, and humidity, and selecting a healthy snake to start with, you'll be setting yourself up for success as a responsible owner. Proper housing and environmental conditions will ensure your ball python has a long, healthy life.

CHAPTER TWO

SETTING UP THE PERFECT ENCLOSURE

Size and Type of Enclosure

Setting up an appropriate enclosure is vital for your ball python's comfort and overall well-being. The right enclosure not only ensures that your snake feels secure but also provides the proper environment for it to thrive.

1. Size of the Enclosure

For a single adult ball python, a 40-gallon tank (or equivalent size in other types of enclosures) is typically recommended. Juvenile snakes can be kept in a smaller 20-gallon tank but will need to upgrade as they grow. The general rule is that the snake's enclosure should be at least as long as the snake's body, ideally offering some extra space for movement.

Recommended Sizes:

Juvenile: 20-30 gallons

Adult: 40 gallons or larger (approximately 36" x 18" x 18")

Ball pythons are not highly active creatures, but they do benefit from the space to explore, hide, and stretch out. An enclosure that is too small can cause stress, leading to potential health issues.

2. Type of Enclosure

Ball pythons can be housed in several types of enclosures:

Glass Tanks: These are the most common and widely available, but they require careful temperature management, as glass is not great at retaining heat and humidity.

Plastic Tubs or Cages: These are often used by breeders due to their easy maintenance and better humidity control.

Wooden Enclosures: These can offer a natural look and provide better insulation for maintaining temperatures. Make sure they have a secure, tight-fitting lid. No matter which type you choose, ensure it is secure, with a properly fitting lid or door to prevent escapes.

SUBSTRATE SELECTION

The substrate you choose for your ball python's enclosure is important for both comfort and hygiene. Ball pythons naturally reside in forests and grasslands, so it's crucial to replicate these conditions as closely as possible to promote healthy shedding and prevent health issues.

Common Substrate Options:

1. Aspen Bedding

Aspen shavings are a popular choice for ball python enclosures. They are lightweight, absorbent, and easy to clean. They also offer a natural look that resembles the snake's natural habitat.

2. Coconut Husk (Coco Fiber)

Coco husk is a great option because it helps to maintain humidity levels while also being a safe and comfortable substrate. It's a little more challenging to clean than aspen, but it's still a good choice for ball pythons.

3. Cypress Mulch

Cypress mulch is another excellent option that holds humidity well and offers a natural look. It's particularly beneficial if you live in a dry climate, as it helps maintain the proper moisture levels.

4. Reptile Carpet

Reptile carpet is reusable and easy to clean, but it doesn't hold moisture or offer the same natural feel as other substrates. It's more commonly used in tanks that need frequent cleaning.

5. Avoid Sand and Gravel

Ball pythons may ingest loose substrates like sand or gravel, which can cause impaction (blockage of the intestines). These types of substrates should be avoided.

Tips for Substrate Care:

• Spot clean daily to remove any waste or uneaten food.

• Replace the substrate completely every 4-6 weeks or as needed based on cleanliness.

• Ensure your substrate does not have sharp edges that could harm your snake.

HEATING AND LIGHTING SETUP

Ball pythons require a controlled temperature range to regulate their body heat properly. The setup of heating and lighting in the enclosure is critical to their health.

1. Heating

Ball pythons need a heat gradient in their enclosure to regulate their body temperature. This can be achieved using different heat sources:

Heat Mats: Place a heat mat under one side of the enclosure to create a warm side. Make sure to use a thermostat to control the temperature and avoid overheating.

Heat Lamps: Heat lamps can be used to create a basking spot for your ball python. Place the lamp above the enclosure to heat the area.

Ceramic Heat Emitters: These emit heat without light and are perfect for creating a warm environment during the nighttime hours.

Temperature Range:

Warm side: 88–92°F (31–33°C)

Cool side: 75–80°F (24–27°C)

Nighttime temperatures: Should not drop below 72°F (22°C). You may need to use a ceramic heat emitter or infrared lamp at night if the room temperature is too low.

2. Lighting

Ball pythons are nocturnal, meaning they don't require intense lighting. Providing a simple low-wattage light for 12 hours a day will help regulate their day-night cycle and support their health. Make sure the light does not add significant heat to the enclosure, as the snake's primary heat source should be from a heat mat or heat lamp.

UVB Lighting: While UVB lighting isn't essential for ball pythons, it can offer benefits, especially in terms of their overall well-being, by encouraging natural behaviors. If you decide to use UVB, a 5.0 UVB bulb is sufficient.

HUMIDITY CONTROL AND WATER NEEDS

Maintaining the right humidity level is essential for your ball python's health, particularly during shedding.

1. Humidity Requirements

Ball pythons thrive in moderate humidity levels, typically between 50% and 60%. During the shedding process, humidity should be increased to around 60–70% to prevent shedding issues.

How to Maintain Humidity:

Misting: Lightly mist the enclosure with water every few days, depending on the humidity level. Avoid excessive misting, as this can create an overly wet environment that can lead to mold or respiratory issues.

Humidity Gauge: Use a hygrometer to keep track of humidity levels in the enclosure. This will help you adjust the environment as needed.

Water Dish: Always provide a clean, shallow water dish large enough for your ball python to soak in. This allows the snake to hydrate and helps with shedding. Change the water regularly to avoid contamination.

2. Soaking for Shedding

Providing a soaking spot during shedding periods helps ball pythons shed more easily. If your snake is having trouble shedding, you can soak it in lukewarm water for 20–30 minutes to aid the process.

HIDES AND ENRICHMENT FEATURES

Hiding spots are essential for your ball python's sense of security and well-being. As a naturally shy snake, it will appreciate having places to retreat to when feeling stressed or vulnerable.

1. Hides

Ball pythons need at least two hides: one on the warm side and one on the cool side of the enclosure. This allows the snake to regulate its body temperature while feeling safe. Ensure the hides are snug, as ball pythons like enclosed spaces that make them feel secure. You can use commercially available hides or create your own using materials like hollow logs or coconut shells.

2. Climbing and Enrichment

Although ball pythons are not highly arboreal, they enjoy having some climbing opportunities. Small branches or logs can be placed inside the enclosure to give your snake a more dynamic environment. A variety of enrichment items such as rocks or cork bark can also add visual interest and provide opportunities for the snake to explore its surroundings.

3. Additional Considerations

Avoid over-furnishing the enclosure. Ball pythons are simple creatures that benefit from a more minimalist approach to enrichment, as too much clutter can stress them out. By setting up the perfect enclosure for your ball python, you'll create an environment where it can thrive. Pay attention to the temperature, humidity, and hiding spaces, and make sure the enclosure reflects the snake's natural habitat. With the right setup, your ball python will have everything it needs to live a long, healthy, and happy life.

FEEDING AND NUTRITION

What to Feed Your Ball Python

Feeding your ball python the right food is essential to its health, growth, and longevity. As obligate carnivores, ball pythons require a diet of whole prey, such as rodents, to meet their nutritional needs.

1. Primary Diet: Rodents

Ball pythons typically eat rodents, with mice and rats being the most common choices. The size of the prey should be appropriate for the size of the snake. Generally, a ball python should eat prey that is no larger than the widest part of its body.

Types of Prey:

Mice: For younger ball pythons and smaller adults, mice are typically the best choice. These can be offered live or frozen/thawed.

Rats: As your ball python grows, it will need larger prey. Rats, both juvenile and adult, are suitable for adult ball pythons.

Other Prey: Occasionally, ball pythons may also be offered other types of prey, such as chicks or rabbits, but rodents should be their primary food source.

2. Nutritional Value

Rodents provide a balanced source of protein, fats, and essential nutrients, including vitamins and minerals. A diet of appropriately sized rodents ensures that your ball python receives the proper nutrition to maintain health.

FEEDING FREQUENCY AND PORTION SIZES

How often you feed your ball python depends on its age, size, and activity level. Younger snakes require more frequent feedings to support their rapid growth, while adults eat less frequently.

1. Juvenile Ball Pythons (under 1 year)

Juvenile ball pythons should be fed once a week. They require smaller prey, typically mice, and should be fed meals that are about the size of the thickest part of their body. At this stage, their growth rate is fast, and they require regular meals to support this growth.

2. Adult Ball Pythons (1 year and older)

Adult ball pythons typically eat once every 7-14 days, depending on their size and activity level. Larger ball pythons may only need to be fed every 10-14 days, while smaller adults may still benefit from weekly feedings. Adults should be offered larger prey, such as rats, which are typically 1.5 to 2 times the size of the snake's girth.

3. Portion Size

A good rule of thumb is to feed your ball python prey that is about the same size as the thickest part of its body. For instance, a snake with a girth of about 1 inch would be fed a prey item that is about 1 inch in diameter.

Juvenile (under 1 year): Mice or rat pups, depending on size

Adult (1 year and older): Small to medium rats, potentially adult rats for larger snakes

4. Adjusting Feeding Frequency

Ball pythons are known for their ability to go without food for extended periods, especially if they are in a cooler environment or during periods of shedding or breeding. It's not uncommon for them to skip a meal occasionally, especially during winter months when their metabolic rate naturally slows down. However, if your ball python refuses food for an extended period (more than a few weeks), it's important to monitor for signs of illness.

LIVE VS FROZEN PREY

When deciding between live or frozen prey, both have their pros and cons. Understanding the differences will help you make the best choice for both you and your ball python.

1. Frozen/Thawed Prey

Frozen prey is a convenient and safe option for feeding your ball python. The main benefits of frozen prey are:

Safety: Frozen prey eliminates the risk of injury that live prey can cause. Live rodents may bite or scratch your snake during feeding, which can lead to infections.

Convenience: Frozen rodents are available in various sizes and are easy to store. You can buy them in bulk, thaw them as needed, and have them ready for feeding.

Nutritional Integrity: When properly frozen and thawed, the nutritional value of the prey remains intact.

To thaw frozen prey, place it in a plastic bag and immerse it in warm water. Never microwave frozen rodents, as this can result in uneven heating and potential harm to your snake. Always make sure the prey is fully thawed before offering it.

2. Live Prey

Some ball pythons may prefer live prey, and feeding live rodents can simulate the natural hunting experience. However, there are several considerations:

Risk of Injury: Live rodents can bite your snake, especially if the snake is slow to strike or miss the target. These injuries can lead to infections and further complications.

Ethical Considerations: Some people prefer frozen prey for ethical reasons, as it avoids the stress of killing live animals.

Prey Escape: Live rodents may escape from the enclosure, causing issues with cleaning and hygiene.

If you choose to feed live prey, be sure to supervise the feeding to ensure that the snake strikes quickly and that the rodent does not pose a threat to the snake.

COMMON FEEDING ISSUES AND SOLUTIONS

Feeding issues are not uncommon when keeping ball pythons, but many can be addressed with the right knowledge and approach.

1. Refusing Food

Ball pythons are known to go off food from time to time. There are several reasons this might happen:

Seasonal Changes: During winter or cooler months, ball pythons may naturally reduce their food intake.

Shedding: Snakes often refuse food when they are about to shed. This is a natural process, and they will resume feeding after shedding.

Stress: Environmental stressors, such as incorrect temperature, humidity, or handling, can cause a ball python to stop eating.

Health Issues: A refusal to eat over an extended period could signal a health issue. If the snake has not eaten for more than a few weeks, it's important to consult a veterinarian.

Solution: Try offering food at different times of the day, adjust temperature or humidity levels, or provide a hiding place for the snake to reduce stress. Always monitor the snake's weight and health closely.

2. Prey Obsession or Overfeeding

Some ball pythons may refuse to stop eating if fed too frequently, or they may become overly aggressive toward their food. Overfeeding can lead to obesity and health problems in the long term.

Solution: Stick to a regular feeding schedule and avoid offering food more frequently than necessary. If your ball python is becoming obsessed with food or showing aggressive behavior toward you, consult a reptile expert or veterinarian.

HANDLING OBESITY AND MALNUTRITION

Proper feeding is essential to ensure your ball python maintains a healthy weight. Both obesity and malnutrition can cause serious health issues.

1. Obesity

Overfeeding is one of the primary causes of obesity in ball pythons. Symptoms include:

An excessively large or bloated body

Difficulty moving or a sluggish demeanor

Loss of muscle tone

Solution: Ensure you are feeding an appropriate size and frequency. If your snake is obese, reduce the portion size and increase the intervals between feedings. Regular exercise can also help maintain a healthy weight.

2. Malnutrition

If a ball python is not fed properly, it may suffer from malnutrition. Signs of malnutrition include:

Weight loss or a noticeable decrease in body mass

Poor shedding

Lethargy

Solution: Ensure that your ball python is getting the right kind of food (whole prey like mice and rats), and adjust its feeding schedule if necessary. If you notice signs of malnutrition, consult a veterinarian immediately. Feeding your ball python is one of the most important aspects of responsible care. By providing a balanced diet, appropriate feeding frequency, and maintaining good feeding practices, you'll ensure that your snake stays healthy and strong for years to come.

CHAPTER THREE

HANDLING AND SOCIALIZATION

How to Handle Your Ball Python Safely

Handling your ball python is an important part of its care, as it allows you to build trust with your pet and ensures that it is comfortable with human interaction. However, it's essential to handle your snake safely and respectfully to avoid stress and potential injury to both you and your ball python.

1. Approaching Your Snake

Before handling, always approach your ball python slowly and calmly. Sudden movements can startle your snake, making it defensive. Let the snake become aware of your presence before attempting to pick it up. Approach from the side, not from above, to mimic natural movements and avoid triggering a defensive strike.

2. Proper Handling Technique

Support the Body: When lifting a ball python, always support its body fully. Hold the snake with one hand near its head and the other near its tail. A good technique is to allow the snake to coil naturally in your hands, providing support for its body's length.

Avoid Gripping: Never grab or squeeze your snake, as this can cause stress and potentially harm it. Handle your ball python gently and allow it to move freely within your hands.

Low to the Ground: When handling, it's advisable to keep the snake close to the ground or on a flat, secure surface. If it escapes your grip, it won't fall far and could potentially injure itself.

3. Handling Frequency

Ball pythons are generally more tolerant of handling than other snake species, but it's important not to overdo it. A few short handling sessions a week are usually sufficient, especially for a new or younger ball python. Over-handling, especially in the early days, can stress the snake and make it hesitant to interact.

4. Handling After Feeding

Avoid handling your ball python immediately after it has eaten, as this can cause stress and lead to regurgitation. Wait at least 48 hours after feeding before attempting to handle your snake.

TIPS FOR REDUCING STRESS IN YOUR SNAKE

Ball pythons are relatively docile snakes, but they can become stressed in certain situations. Reducing stress is crucial for their health and well-being. Here are some tips to minimize stress:

1. Maintain a Consistent Environment

Stress often occurs when there are sudden changes in the snake's environment. Ensure that your ball python's habitat has stable temperature and humidity levels. Keeping the enclosure clean and free of strong odors is also essential.

2. Avoid Over-Handling

While handling is important for bonding, too much of it can stress your snake. Let your ball python settle into its new environment before beginning regular handling. A snake that's over-handled may become stressed and even more defensive.

3. Provide Hides and Retreat Spaces

Ball pythons feel safer when they have places to hide. Make sure your snake has access to one or more hides that offer a sense of security. Providing dark, snug spaces in its enclosure will reduce stress, as it can retreat whenever it feels threatened.

4. Quiet, Calm Surroundings

Keeping your ball python in a calm, quiet area of the home will prevent overstimulation from noise or movement. Avoid placing the enclosure in areas with frequent traffic or loud noises.

5. Limit Handling When Shedding or Sick

During shedding or if your ball python is sick, minimize handling to reduce stress. These times can be physically taxing on your snake, and handling can interfere with its natural behaviors.

UNDERSTANDING BALL PYTHON BEHAVIOR

To provide the best care for your ball python, it's important to understand its natural behaviors. These behaviors reflect its comfort level, mood, and overall health. Here are some common behavioral cues and what they mean:

1. Curled Up (Ball Position)

Ball pythons are known for curling into a tight ball when they feel threatened. This behavior is a defensive mechanism, where they wrap their body and hide their head to protect themselves. If your ball python is curled up, it may be stressed, frightened, or simply resting.

2. Exploration

Ball pythons are generally curious animals. They may spend a significant amount of time exploring their enclosure, especially when first introduced. This is a normal behavior as they familiarize themselves with their surroundings.

3. Tongue Flicking

Snakes use their forked tongue to "taste" the air, picking up chemical cues. Frequent tongue flicking is normal and a sign that your ball python is active and trying to understand its environment. It may flick its tongue more when investigating new objects or potential prey.

4. Striking Behavior

Ball pythons may strike if they feel threatened or when they are hungry. Unlike other snakes, ball pythons are not typically aggressive, and their strikes are often a defensive reaction. If your snake strikes, it's important to assess whether it feels stressed or threatened by its environment or handling.

5. Defensive Hissing

A ball python may hiss as a warning sign if it feels threatened. It's a way for the snake to signal that it's not in the mood to interact. Hissing can also occur if the snake feels uncomfortable with its surroundings, such as the temperature or humidity being off.

BONDING WITH YOUR BALL PYTHON

While ball pythons aren't social creatures in the same way some other pets are, they can form a bond with their owners over time. The key to bonding with your snake is patience, consistency, and respect.

1. Take It Slow

Ball pythons don't bond instantly, so it's important to give them time to adjust to their environment and to your presence. If you're new to snake care, start by simply sitting near the enclosure to let your ball python become accustomed to you before attempting any handling.

2. Frequent, Gentle Handling

Over time, handling your ball python in a calm and consistent manner will help build trust. Start with short sessions and gradually increase the duration. If your snake seems stressed, cut the session short and try again later.

3. Observe Body Language

Pay attention to your snake's body language during handling. If it shows signs of stress (such as tight coiling or rapid flicking of its tongue), it may need a break. Respect its comfort level and give it time to adjust.

4. Offer Food by Hand

Occasionally offering food by hand can help establish trust. If your ball python eats from your hand, it's a good sign that it associates you with positive experiences. This can help strengthen the bond between you and your pet. Handling and socializing with your ball python is a gradual process that requires patience and consistency. By understanding your snake's behavior, reducing stress, and building trust through gentle handling, you can create a positive and lasting relationship with your pet.

HEALTH AND HYGIENE

Signs of a Healthy Ball Python

Keeping your ball python healthy is crucial for its well-being, and being able to identify signs of a healthy snake can help you ensure that your pet thrives. Here are the key signs to look for:

1. Clear Eyes

A healthy ball python should have clear, bright eyes with no cloudiness or swelling. Cloudy eyes can indicate a health issue, such as dehydration or infection, especially during shedding.

2. Glossy, Smooth Skin

Ball pythons should have smooth, glossy skin. Any rough or patchy skin could be a sign of illness or a shedding problem. Healthy skin is typically a consistent color, with no lesions, bumps, or scars.

3. Good Appetite

A healthy ball python will readily eat. While snakes have varying appetites depending on age and season, a consistent lack of interest in food may indicate an underlying health issue.

4. Active and Alert

Healthy ball pythons are usually active, especially at night when they are most active in the wild. They should be alert when you approach their enclosure, flicking their tongues to explore their surroundings.

5. Proper Weight

A healthy ball python should have a proportional body length and weight. If your snake is too thin or too heavy, it could be an indication of malnutrition, obesity, or other health concerns.

6. Consistent Shedding

Ball pythons should shed regularly as they grow. A snake that sheds in one complete piece with no retained skin is typically healthy. Partial or problematic shedding may indicate an issue with humidity, hydration, or skin health.

COMMON DISEASES AND CONDITIONS

Like any pet, ball pythons are susceptible to a range of health issues. Understanding common diseases and conditions can help you detect problems early and seek treatment promptly.

1. Respiratory Infections (RI)

Respiratory infections are common in ball pythons and can be caused by poor husbandry, such as inadequate temperature or humidity levels. Symptoms include wheezing, open-mouth breathing, nasal discharge, or a bubbly mouth. If left untreated, respiratory infections can be fatal.

Prevention/Treatment: Ensure proper temperature and humidity levels, and consult a vet for antibiotics if your snake shows symptoms.

2. Scale Rot (Infectious Dermatitis)

Scale rot is a bacterial infection that affects the skin, causing the scales to become damaged, discolored, or ulcerated. It is often the result of poor enclosure hygiene or excessive moisture in the substrate.

Prevention/Treatment: Keep the enclosure clean and dry. If scale rot occurs, consult a vet for topical treatments or antibiotics.

3. Mites and Parasites

Mites are tiny external parasites that can infest your ball python's skin, causing irritation and discomfort. Symptoms of a mite infestation include excessive rubbing, skin discoloration, or visible dark specks around the eyes and body.

Prevention/Treatment: Regularly inspect your snake for signs of parasites and maintain a clean enclosure. If you detect mites, a veterinarian can provide treatment, such as mite-killing sprays or baths.

4. Obesity

Overfeeding or feeding prey that is too large can lead to obesity in ball pythons. An overweight snake is at higher risk for other health issues, such as respiratory problems, heart issues, and difficulty shedding.

Prevention/Treatment: Feed your snake an appropriate-sized meal and monitor its weight. If your ball python is obese, adjust its diet and feeding schedule, and consult a vet for advice.

5. Infections and Abscesses

Infections, often caused by wounds or poor enclosure conditions, can lead to abscesses. These are typically visible as lumps under the skin, often with a pus-filled center. Abscesses can become severe if untreated.

Prevention/Treatment: Maintain a clean environment and inspect your snake for injuries regularly. If an abscess occurs, seek immediate veterinary attention.

PREVENTATIVE CARE AND REGULAR CHECKUPS

Preventative care is essential in maintaining your ball python's health. By staying proactive and addressing small issues before they become big problems, you can ensure your snake remains healthy for years to come.

1. Regular Health Checks

Even if your snake appears healthy, routine checkups with a reptile veterinarian are important. A vet can perform an overall health assessment, check for internal parasites, and provide advice on diet, enclosure setup, and general care.

2. Proper Husbandry

The foundation of a healthy ball python is proper husbandry. Maintaining the right temperature, humidity, and lighting, along with providing a clean and safe environment, will help your snake stay healthy and prevent many common health issues.

3. Parasite Prevention

Regularly inspect your ball python for signs of external parasites like mites, ticks, and lice. Make sure to quarantine any new snakes you introduce to prevent the spread of parasites or diseases.

4. Diet and Nutrition

Providing a balanced diet is essential to your ball python's health. Ensure you're offering appropriately sized meals and avoid overfeeding. Proper feeding practices will prevent obesity and support healthy growth.

5. Shedding Health

Ensure your snake has adequate humidity and hydration to shed properly. If shedding issues persist, a vet may provide advice or treatment to ensure your ball python sheds in one complete piece.

CLEANING AND MAINTAINING THE ENCLOSURE

Keeping your ball python's enclosure clean is essential for its health. A clean habitat reduces the risk of infections, parasites, and stress. Here's how to maintain a hygienic enclosure:

1. Spot Clean Daily

Remove any uneaten food, waste, or substrate that may be soiled. Spot cleaning daily helps prevent bacteria build-up and ensures a pleasant environment for your snake.

2. Full Enclosure Clean Weekly

Once a week, thoroughly clean the entire enclosure. Remove all substrate and replace it with fresh bedding. Clean all surfaces with a reptile-safe disinfectant, and wash all water dishes to prevent bacterial growth.

3. Check Humidity Levels

Regularly check the humidity levels in your ball python's enclosure, as improper humidity can lead to health problems. Adjust the humidity as needed by misting the enclosure or adjusting the water dish placement.

4. Maintain Temperature Consistency

Make sure the temperature gradient in the enclosure is consistent. Use a thermometer to monitor the warm and cool zones of the habitat, ensuring they stay within the ideal range for your snake.

DEALING WITH SHEDDING ISSUES

Shedding is a natural and necessary part of a ball python's life cycle, but sometimes shedding issues can occur. Here's what to do if your snake experiences problems with shedding:

1. Dehydration and Low Humidity

One of the most common causes of shedding issues is inadequate humidity. Ensure that the humidity in the enclosure is between 50-60%, and provide a humidity box or moist hide during shedding periods to help the snake.

2. Retained Eye Caps

Ball pythons sometimes retain the skin around their eyes, which can lead to issues with vision and health. If you notice that your snake's eye caps are retained, increase humidity and gently rub the affected area with a damp cloth.

3. Partial Shedding

Partial shedding can occur due to dehydration or environmental stress. If your ball python is shedding in pieces or retaining skin on its body, you can help by soaking it in a shallow, lukewarm water bath for around 20 minutes. This can soften the skin and encourage the snake to shed it.

4. Consult a Vet

If your snake continues to have shedding problems or experiences pain while shedding, it's time to consult a veterinarian. They can help identify the underlying cause of the shedding issues and provide treatment.

Maintaining good health and hygiene is fundamental for your ball python's long-term happiness. By providing a clean, stable environment and being vigilant about health concerns, you can help your snake thrive. Regular checkups, good husbandry practices, and prompt attention to health issues will ensure your ball python remains healthy and active.

CHAPTER FOUR

BALL PYTHON BREEDING BASICS

Understanding the Reproductive Cycle of Ball Pythons

Ball pythons, like many reptiles, have a seasonal reproductive cycle. Their breeding behavior is influenced by environmental cues such as temperature, humidity, and light, which mimic the dry and wet seasons in their native habitat. Understanding this cycle is key to successful breeding.

1. Mating Season

Ball pythons breed during a specific time of year, typically between November and March. During this period, males become more active in seeking out females, and the females may be more receptive to mating. Outside of this window, both males and females tend to be less active in terms of reproductive behavior.

2. Hibernation/Brumation Period

Before breeding, male ball pythons may go through a period of brumation, where their activity levels decrease. This is similar to hibernation in mammals but not as intense. It is thought that a period of slightly cooler temperatures and lower activity helps stimulate the reproductive cycle.

3. Female Reproductive Cycle

Female ball pythons go through a period of follicular development, where eggs are formed inside their ovaries. This stage is key for breeding, as a female will only be receptive to males when her follicles are sufficiently developed, which happens just before ovulation.

4. Ovulation

Ovulation occurs when the female's eggs are released and are ready to be fertilized. Ovulation is a critical event in the breeding cycle and is typically preceded by a noticeable increase in the size of the female's belly as the follicles mature. The best time to introduce the male is when ovulation is imminent.

CHOOSING BREEDING PAIRS

Selecting the right breeding pair is crucial for producing healthy offspring. The decision depends on various factors, including genetics, health, and temperament.

1. Genetics and Morphs

One of the most exciting aspects of breeding ball pythons is the wide range of morphs and color patterns. Many breeders choose pairs based on the desired genetic traits to produce particular morphs. However, it's important to also consider genetic diversity to avoid inbreeding, which can lead to health issues in offspring.

2. Health of the Parents

Both the male and female should be in excellent health before breeding. They should be disease-free and of appropriate size and age. A healthy snake is one that has been well-fed, has shed properly, and has no visible signs of illness or injury.

3. Age and Size of the Pair

Female ball pythons typically reach sexual maturity around 2-3 years of age and should be at least 1,500 grams before breeding. Males can breed earlier but should also be of sufficient size (around 500 grams) and maturity. Breeding snakes that are too young or too small can result in complications.

4. Temperament

It's important to observe the behavior of both the male and female before pairing them. While ball pythons are generally docile, some snakes may be more aggressive during breeding. Ensure that both snakes are calm and not showing signs of stress or aggression.

PREPARING FOR BREEDING SEASON

Before attempting to breed, proper preparation is key. This ensures that both the male and female are in peak condition, and the breeding environment is optimal.

1. Temperature and Humidity

Gradually lower the temperature in the enclosure to simulate the cooler months of their native habitat. This decrease in temperature (around 75-80°F or 24-27°C) signals the approach of the breeding season. The humidity should also be adjusted to mirror their natural wet and dry seasons, with a slight increase to around 60-70% during the breeding season.

2. Feeding

Prior to breeding, both the male and female should be in excellent nutritional condition. Provide them with high-quality food, and ensure that they are well-fed but not overweight. It's recommended to feed females a slightly higher quantity before the breeding season to ensure they have enough energy reserves for ovulation and egg production.

3. Introducing the Pair

Introduce the male to the female once you notice signs that the female is receptive, usually when she is in the pre-ovulation stage. Keep the introductions brief and observe their behavior. If the female shows signs of aggression or stress, separate them and try again after a few days.

4. Environmental Enrichment

During the breeding season, ensure the snakes have a suitable environment for mating. This includes providing adequate hides, substrate for burrowing, and a quiet, stress-free area. Avoid excessive handling during this time to allow the snakes to focus on reproduction.

MANAGING MATING AND OVULATION

The mating process can take several weeks, and it's important to manage the environment and behavior of your breeding pair carefully during this time.

1. Mating Rituals

The male will begin to court the female by rubbing his chin on her body, flicking his tongue, and performing a "locking" behavior. This occurs when the male inserts his hemipenes into the female's cloaca. Successful mating may take several attempts, and sometimes, the male will mate with the female multiple times.

2. Observing Mating Success

After mating, it's important to monitor the female's behavior and physical condition. You should notice a slight swelling in her abdomen as the follicles begin to develop and prepare for ovulation. If the mating is successful, the female will begin to show signs of ovulation within a few weeks.

3. Ovulation Indicators

Ovulation is a significant event in the reproductive cycle. You can usually detect ovulation by the female's enlarged abdomen and the presence of large follicles. This is when the female is most fertile, and it's the ideal time for egg fertilization. Keep track of the female's progress and ensure she is in optimal conditions for ovulation.

4. Post-Mating Care

After mating, it's essential to continue providing the female with the correct environmental conditions. Keep her in a calm, low-stress environment and monitor her for any signs of illness. During ovulation, the female may refuse food, which is normal. If she shows any signs of distress or abnormal behavior, consult a veterinarian.

INCUBATING EGGS

Once the female has laid her eggs, proper incubation is crucial for successful hatching. Here's how to ensure that your ball python eggs develop correctly:

1. Egg Laying

Female ball pythons typically lay 4 to 10 eggs per clutch, although this can vary. Once the eggs are laid, the female may remain with them for several weeks. It's important to remove the eggs once the female is no longer guarding them.

2. Incubator Setup

For successful incubation, you'll need a reliable incubator that can maintain a consistent temperature of around 88-90°F (31-32°C) and humidity around 60-70%. A reptile egg incubator with adjustable temperature controls is ideal. The eggs should be placed in an incubator with moist, vermiculite or perlite substrate to maintain humidity.

3. Monitoring Eggs

Regularly check the temperature and humidity in the incubator to ensure they stay within the ideal range. Gently turn the eggs every few days to prevent them from sticking to the sides of the container. Avoid disturbing the eggs too much, as this can cause stress or disrupt their development.

4. Hatching

Ball python eggs typically incubate for 55-60 days before hatching. As the hatchlings near their due date, you may see small cracks or holes in the eggs as they begin to break out. Once the hatchlings emerge, provide them with a suitable environment for the first few weeks of life.

Breeding ball pythons is a rewarding and exciting process, but it requires careful preparation, observation, and attention to detail. By understanding the reproductive cycle, selecting the right pairs, managing the mating process, and ensuring proper incubation, you can successfully breed healthy and thriving ball pythons.

ADVANCED BREEDING TECHNIQUES

Selective Breeding and Morphs

Selective breeding is a key strategy for ball python breeders aiming to produce specific traits, colors, and patterns in their offspring. This practice involves choosing breeding pairs with desirable traits to enhance the chances of passing those traits down to the next generation.

1. What is Selective Breeding?

Selective breeding involves pairing snakes with particular genetic traits, such as color morphs, pattern changes, or other unique characteristics. By selecting breeding pairs with specific traits, breeders can increase the likelihood of producing offspring with those same traits. Over time, this can lead to the development of new morphs or color variations that are more visually appealing to buyers or collectors.

2. Popular Ball Python Morphs

Some of the most popular morphs in ball pythons include:

Albino: Known for their bright yellow and white coloration.

Pied: A pattern morph with white and color patches.

Clown: Features a distinctive pattern with darker colors.

Banana: Known for its yellow, spotted pattern and purple hues.

These morphs are produced by combining specific genetic traits, and breeders often select parents based on the likelihood of producing offspring with these traits.

3. Ethical Considerations

When engaging in selective breeding, it's important to maintain a focus on the health and welfare of the snakes. Genetic diversity should always be maintained to avoid inbreeding, which can lead to health problems. Additionally, breeders should be mindful of the ethical implications of breeding for appearance over health and temperament.

GENETIC CONSIDERATIONS IN BALL PYTHON BREEDING

Genetics plays a significant role in the success of ball python breeding. Understanding how genes influence physical traits, such as color and pattern, can help breeders predict offspring characteristics.

1. Dominant vs. Recessive Traits

Dominant Traits: These traits are expressed in the offspring if at least one parent carries the gene for that trait. For example, the Pied morph is a dominant trait, meaning that a ball python only needs one Pied parent to produce Pied offspring.

Recessive Traits: These traits are only expressed when both parents carry the recessive gene. Traits like Albino and Clown are recessive, meaning that two carriers must be paired to produce offspring with these morphs.

2. Co-dominant Traits

Co-dominant traits are a special category where both alleles are expressed in the offspring. A good example is the Mojave morph, where both the Mojave gene and a normal gene will produce offspring with a unique appearance.

3. Breeding for Specific Traits

By understanding genetic inheritance, breeders can plan pairings to achieve specific morph combinations. However, this requires knowledge of how genes interact and careful record-keeping to track the genetic history of each animal.

4. Avoiding Inbreeding

Inbreeding, or breeding closely related animals, can result in health problems and reduced vitality in offspring. It's crucial to pair snakes from different genetic lines to ensure genetic diversity and healthy offspring.

MANAGING MULTIPLE BREEDING PAIRS

Managing multiple breeding pairs requires a strategic approach, as the care and attention given to each pair can vary depending on their needs.

Here are some tips for handling multiple breeding pairs effectively:

1. Space Management

If you are breeding several pairs, it's important to have enough space for each pair to have their own separate enclosures. This minimizes stress and ensures that each pair has the right environmental conditions for successful breeding. Avoid overcrowding, as this can cause territorial disputes or reduce breeding success.

2. Tracking Breeding Cycles

Keeping track of the reproductive cycles of each pair is essential for successful breeding. Use a breeding calendar or spreadsheet to monitor when each pair mates, when the female is due to ovulate, and when eggs are expected. This helps you plan for incubation and ensures that each pair is properly managed throughout the season.

3. Male Rotation

If you have several females but only one male, consider rotating the male between different females. This allows the male to breed with multiple females without becoming too stressed or worn out. Ensure that the male is healthy and has access to proper nutrition during this time.

4. Health Monitoring

When managing multiple pairs, regular health checks are essential. Monitor for signs of illness or stress in both males and females, especially during the breeding season when they may be more susceptible to infections or injury.

INCUBATION AND HATCHING TIPS

Once the eggs are laid, successful incubation and hatching require careful attention to temperature, humidity, and egg handling. Here's how to increase the chances of successful hatching:

1. Incubator Setup

A reliable incubator is essential for maintaining the right conditions. Set the temperature to 88-90°F (31-32°C), and ensure that humidity levels are around 60-70%. Use a digital thermometer and hygrometer to constantly monitor the environment. Make sure the eggs are in a secure container with ventilation holes to allow for air circulation.

2. Egg Handling

Once the female has laid her eggs, carefully remove them from the substrate and place them in an incubator. It's important to handle the eggs gently, as they are delicate. If the eggs are attached to each other, do not try to separate them. Simply place them in the incubator as they are.

3. Turning the Eggs

Turn the eggs gently every 2-3 days to prevent them from sticking to the container. If you notice any mold or discoloration, remove the affected eggs immediately. Some breeders choose to mark the tops of the eggs to ensure they are positioned correctly during incubation.

4. Hatchling Care

As the eggs near hatching, monitor them carefully. Hatchlings usually begin to crack the egg around the 55-60 day mark. Once they have emerged, do not rush to handle them. Allow the hatchlings to absorb the yolk sac and shed for the first time. Afterward, provide them with a suitable enclosure and begin feeding them.

RAISING HEALTHY HATCHLINGS

Raising healthy hatchlings is a rewarding process that requires proper care and attention. Here's how to ensure the best start for your baby ball pythons:

1. Initial Care

After hatching, the first few weeks are critical for hatchlings. Set them up in small, secure enclosures with appropriate temperature and humidity levels. Hatchlings are more vulnerable to stress, so minimize handling during this time.

2. Feeding Hatchlings

Most hatchlings will take their first meal 1-2 weeks after hatching, often starting with smaller prey items like pinky mice or appropriately sized rats. Ensure that the food is pre-killed or frozen-thawed to reduce the risk of injury.

3. Monitoring Growth

Keep a close eye on the hatchlings' growth. Healthy hatchlings should gain weight steadily and shed regularly. If you notice any issues with feeding or weight loss, consult a reptile veterinarian for advice.

4. Sexing and Selling

As the hatchlings grow, you may begin to sex them. It's important to wait until they are old enough to accurately determine their sex, usually at 6-12 months. Once they are established, you can begin selling or keeping them for future breeding.

By utilizing advanced breeding techniques like selective breeding, understanding genetic inheritance, managing multiple pairs effectively, and following best practices for incubation and hatchling care, breeders can produce healthy, thriving ball pythons that are sought after for their unique traits and morphs. This chapter has provided insight into some of the most important aspects of advanced breeding, allowing you to refine your breeding program and increase your success in the world of ball pythons.

CHAPTER FIVE

COMMON BREEDING CHALLENGES

Breeding ball pythons can be a rewarding endeavor, but it comes with its fair share of challenges. From infertility issues to managing hatchling health, breeders must be prepared to troubleshoot and address any difficulties that arise. This chapter covers some of the most common breeding challenges, along with strategies for handling them effectively.

COPING WITH INFERTILITY ISSUES

Infertility can be a frustrating issue for breeders, especially when the pairing seems ideal, yet the female does not produce eggs. There are several reasons why infertility might occur in ball pythons:

1. Unhealthy Mating Pair

One of the most common causes of infertility is an unhealthy or underprepared mating pair. Ensure that both the male and female are in optimal health before beginning the breeding process. Poor nutrition, inadequate housing, or stress can all contribute to infertility.

2. Improper Breeding Conditions

Ball pythons are sensitive to environmental factors such as temperature, humidity, and light cycles. If these conditions are not optimal, it can negatively impact fertility. Females may not ovulate, or they may lay infertile eggs. Proper temperature gradients and humidity levels are critical throughout the breeding season.

3. Male Fertility Issues

Male infertility is less common but can occur. If the male is not producing viable sperm, he may need a break or additional care to restore fertility.

Low sperm count or poor sperm quality can result in unsuccessful matings. Consider rotating males or pairing them with females at different times to give them a break from the breeding season.

4. Nutritional Deficiencies

Both males and females require a balanced diet to maintain fertility. Ensure that your snakes are getting enough of the right nutrients, particularly during the breeding season. Offer high-quality prey, and consider supplementation with vitamins and minerals if necessary.

5. Age and Health of Female

Female ball pythons that are too young or too old may have difficulty producing eggs. Most females are ready to breed around 2-4 years of age, but this can vary based on individual health and size. Breeding too early or too late can lead to infertility or health complications.

Solutions for Infertility:

• Ensure optimal breeding conditions with proper temperatures, humidity, and light cycles.

• Provide a nutritious, varied diet to support reproductive health.

• Monitor the health of both the male and female closely and consult a veterinarian if needed.

• Consider rotating males if you suspect male fertility issues.

DEALING WITH EGG BINDING

Egg binding, also known as dystocia, is a serious condition where a female ball python is unable to lay her eggs. This condition can be life-threatening if not addressed promptly, and it can occur for various reasons:

1. Size of the Eggs

One common cause of egg binding is that the eggs are too large for the female to pass. This often occurs in females that are underprepared or in poor health.

2. Low Temperatures or Poor Enclosure Conditions

A female's ability to lay eggs can be severely affected by low temperatures or inadequate humidity. If the environmental conditions aren't suitable, the female may not be able to pass the eggs, leading to egg retention.

3. Stress or Inadequate Space

Excessive stress from handling or being housed in a cramped enclosure can interfere with the laying process. Females need a quiet, secure place to lay their eggs.

4. Underlying Health Issues

Egg binding can also be a result of underlying health problems, such as infections, hormonal imbalances, or insufficient calcium. If a female is not healthy, she may be unable to lay eggs properly.

Signs of Egg Binding:

• Swollen abdomen or visible lumps in the body.

• Difficulty moving or exhibiting signs of distress.

• Visible straining but no eggs being laid.

Solutions for Egg Binding:

• Immediate Veterinary Care: Egg binding requires professional intervention. A veterinarian can often assist with removing the eggs manually or through other medical procedures if necessary.

• Supportive Care: If the binding is mild, supportive care such as increasing the temperature and humidity in the enclosure may help the female pass the eggs naturally.

• Preventative Measures: To prevent egg binding, ensure that females are in optimal health before breeding, provide appropriate nesting sites, and maintain the right environmental conditions.

MANAGING HATCHLING CARE AND HEALTH

After successfully breeding and hatching ball pythons, the next challenge is raising healthy hatchlings. While most hatchlings will thrive with proper care, there are some common issues that breeders may encounter during this stage:

1. Refusing to Eat

Hatchlings sometimes refuse to eat after hatching, especially during their first few weeks. This is common, but it can be frustrating for breeders. The stress of hatching, changes in the environment, or the absence of proper prey can all contribute to feeding problems.

Solution: Try offering freshly thawed, appropriately sized prey. Some hatchlings may need time to adjust to their new environment, so patience is key. If they continue to refuse food for extended periods, consult a veterinarian for guidance.

2. Dehydration and Shedding Issues

Dehydration can lead to complications such as shedding problems. Hatchlings may struggle to shed their skin properly, which can cause retained shed. This condition is uncomfortable and can lead to infections if not addressed.

Solution: Ensure that hatchlings have access to fresh water at all times. Maintain appropriate humidity levels in their enclosures, especially when they are nearing a shed cycle. If a hatchling has retained shed, gently mist the enclosure to help with the shedding process, or consult a vet for further treatment.

3. Injury or Cannibalism

Although rare, hatchlings may injure each other or engage in cannibalistic behavior. This can happen if there are too many hatchlings in one enclosure or if one snake is particularly weak or sickly.

Solution: Separate hatchlings that seem weak or at risk from the others. Provide enough space in the enclosure to reduce stress and competition. Monitor them closely during their first few weeks of life.

4. Health Monitoring

Hatchlings need regular health checkups to ensure they are growing properly and are free from infections or parasites. Their small size and vulnerability make them more susceptible to illnesses, so keep a close eye on their eating habits, weight gain, and behavior.

Solution: Track each hatchling's weight and growth over time. If you notice any signs of illness or stunted growth, take them to a veterinarian for evaluation and treatment.

TROUBLESHOOTING BREEDING PROBLEMS

Despite the best planning, breeders may encounter issues during the breeding process. Troubleshooting these problems is essential to ensure a successful breeding season.

1. Mating Inactivity

Sometimes, even with perfect conditions, a male ball python may show little interest in mating. This could be due to stress, improper temperatures, or even simply an issue with the male's fertility.

Solution: Ensure the breeding area is calm and free from disturbances. Increase the male's exposure to the female, but don't force the process. If the male continues to show disinterest, consider rotating him out for a few weeks to give him a break, or use a different male.

2. Female Not Ovulating

If the female does not ovulate despite multiple attempts at breeding, it could be due to improper environmental conditions, nutritional deficiencies, or stress.

Solution: Reevaluate the environmental setup, paying special attention to temperature and humidity levels. Ensure the female is in optimal health and has received the proper diet leading up to the breeding season.

3. Laying Infertile Eggs

Occasionally, a female may lay eggs that are infertile, meaning they were never fertilized by the male. This can be caused by poor timing or issues with male fertility.

Solution: Consider adjusting the timing of the pairings to ensure that the male is properly engaging with the female at the right time. If this is a consistent issue, evaluate the health and fertility of the male. By understanding and addressing common breeding challenges such as infertility, egg binding, hatchling care, and other breeding issues, breeders can improve their success rates and ensure the health and well-being of their ball pythons throughout the breeding process. With patience, knowledge, and the right resources, you can navigate these challenges and produce thriving ball pythons.

CREATING A SUCCESSFUL BALL PYTHON BREEDING PROGRAM

Building a successful ball python breeding program takes more than just pairing snakes and hoping for hatchlings. It requires careful planning, tracking, and continuous learning. A well-organized breeding program can not only enhance the quality and health of your snakes but also establish a solid reputation within the reptile breeding community. This chapter will guide you through the steps needed to create a successful and sustainable breeding program.

SETTING GOALS FOR YOUR BREEDING PROGRAM

The first step in creating a successful breeding program is setting clear, realistic goals. Without a solid vision for your breeding endeavors, it can be easy to lose focus and direction. Your goals will help shape your breeding strategies, whether you aim to produce specific morphs, improve the overall health and vitality of your snakes, or increase the size and diversity of your breeding stock.

1. Identify Your Focus

Do you want to specialize in a specific morph or type of ball python, or are you more interested in improving the overall genetic diversity of your breeding stock? Setting a clear focus will help guide the pairings you select and determine which snakes you add to your collection.

2. Quality Over Quantity

It's tempting to focus on producing a large number of hatchlings, but prioritizing quality is key to building a reputable breeding program. Aim for producing well-adjusted, healthy, and genetically strong snakes rather than focusing on sheer volume. This approach will ensure that your ball pythons stand out in the marketplace and attract long-term success.

3. Plan for Long-Term Success

Establish short-term and long-term breeding goals. For example, you may set a goal to produce a specific morph within two breeding seasons, while over the next 5-10 years, you may aim to build a larger breeding stock that allows for consistent genetic diversity.

TRACKING GENETICS AND LINEAGE

One of the most crucial aspects of breeding ball pythons is understanding and tracking their genetics. Ball pythons are known for their stunning array of morphs, which are the result of genetic mutations. To ensure the health and quality of your breeding program, it's essential to track the lineage and genetics of every snake in your collection.

1. Understanding Morphs and Genetics

Different morphs of ball pythons are the result of specific genetic mutations. Some mutations are recessive, meaning both parents must carry the gene for the morph to be expressed, while others are dominant or co-dominant, which only require one parent to carry the gene for the trait to appear. Understanding these genetic traits will allow you to make informed decisions when selecting breeding pairs.

2. Creating a Genetic Database

Keeping detailed records of the genetics and lineage of your snakes is essential for tracking potential inbreeding and maintaining genetic diversity. This can be done manually in a breeding notebook or digitally using breeding software or spreadsheets. Make sure to document:

The morphs and genetic traits of each snake

The parents and offspring of each individual snake

Any health issues or notable characteristics

3. Avoiding Inbreeding

Inbreeding can lead to genetic defects and health issues in ball pythons. By tracking lineage and keeping detailed records, you can avoid breeding closely related snakes and ensure that your breeding program remains diverse and healthy. Consider rotating males and adding new bloodlines to maintain genetic strength and diversity.

4. Utilizing Pedigree Information

In a serious breeding program, pedigree information can add value. Ball python breeders may seek snakes with prestigious bloodlines to enhance their breeding stock, so knowing the pedigree of each snake in your program will give you an edge in the market.

KEEPING DETAILED RECORDS

Accurate record-keeping is crucial for the success of any breeding program. Not only does it help you track genetics, but it also provides insights into breeding patterns, health trends, and growth rates. Keeping detailed records will also help you troubleshoot any breeding issues and improve future breeding decisions.

1. Breeding Logs

For each pairing, create a breeding log that includes:

The date of pairing and frequency of matings

The health and condition of both the male and female

Any observable signs of ovulation or mating success

The date of egg-laying and incubation periods

Hatchling counts and any issues during hatching

2. Health and Care Records

Keep track of health records for each snake in your collection, including vaccinations, health check-ups, and any treatments for illnesses or injuries. Record their feeding schedules and any changes in appetite or behavior, which could indicate health problems.

3. Growth and Development Logs

Track the growth of hatchlings over time to monitor their health and ensure they are developing as expected. Record their feeding habits, weight, and any issues with shedding, as these can be indicative of underlying health concerns.

4. Financial Records

It's important to track the financial aspects of your breeding program as well, including the costs of feeding, housing, veterinary care, and any other expenses related to breeding. This will help you assess the profitability of your breeding program and guide you in making informed decisions about scaling your operations.

MARKETING AND SELLING HATCHLINGS

Once your ball pythons have hatched and are ready to be sold, it's time to focus on marketing and selling your hatchlings. Building a strong reputation and maintaining ethical breeding practices are key to success in the reptile marketplace. Here are some steps for effectively marketing and selling your ball pythons:

1. Building a Brand

Establish your brand as a reliable, ethical breeder of high-quality ball pythons. This includes maintaining a professional online presence, providing excellent customer service, and educating potential buyers about the care and genetics of your snakes.

2. Utilizing Online Platforms

Online reptile forums, Facebook groups, and marketplace platforms like MorphMarket are popular places for ball python breeders to sell their hatchlings. Create detailed listings with high-quality photos, clear descriptions, and information about the snake's genetics, health, and temperament.

3. Networking with Other Breeders and Enthusiasts

Building relationships with other breeders, enthusiasts, and reptile shops can help you sell your hatchlings more effectively. Attend reptile expos, trade shows, and local reptile clubs to meet potential buyers and establish connections with others in the industry.

4. Pricing Your Hatchlings

Pricing your ball pythons depends on factors such as morph rarity, genetic quality, and market demand. Keep in mind that higher-quality morphs or rare genetic combinations can command higher prices, but it's essential to price your snakes competitively and ethically. Research the current market prices and avoid overpricing, as this could turn potential buyers away.

5. Customer Education and Support

Providing buyers with educational resources and support after the sale is crucial for ensuring the long-term care and health of your snakes. Offer advice on feeding, housing, and general care, and make yourself available to answer questions post-sale. Happy customers are likely to return or recommend your breeding program to others. By setting clear goals, tracking genetics, keeping thorough records, and effectively marketing your hatchlings, you can create a successful and sustainable ball python breeding program. It takes time, effort, and commitment, but the rewards of producing healthy, high-quality snakes and building a reputation within the breeding community are well worth the investment. Whether you're aiming for a hobbyist collection or a professional breeding business, this chapter provides the essential building blocks for your success.

CHAPTER SIX

ETHICAL CONSIDERATIONS IN BALL PYTHON BREEDING

Ethics plays a pivotal role in every aspect of animal breeding, including ball python breeding. As a responsible breeder, it's essential to prioritize the well-being of the animals and consider the impact of your breeding practices on the overall ball python population and ecosystem. This chapter will explore key ethical considerations that every breeder should keep in mind to ensure that their breeding practices are both responsible and sustainable.

BREEDING FOR THE RIGHT REASONS

Ball python breeding can be an exciting and rewarding venture, but it's essential to approach it for the right reasons. Breeding should not only be about financial gain or the pursuit of rare morphs. True ethical breeding is centered around improving the health and well-being of the species, conserving their genetic diversity, and providing future owners with healthy, well-cared-for snakes.

1. Health and Well-being First

Ethical breeders prioritize the health of their snakes above all else. This means focusing on the overall genetic quality of your breeding stock, not just rare or exotic morphs. Health should be the primary consideration when selecting breeding pairs to ensure that they are free from inherited diseases and genetic defects.

2. Conservation and Sustainability

Responsible breeders also consider the conservation of ball pythons in the wild. While ball pythons are widely bred in captivity, ensuring that your breeding practices don't contribute to the depletion of wild populations is important. Breeding for genetic diversity can help preserve the species and prevent inbreeding, which can lead to long-term health problems.

3. Avoiding Over-Breeding

Ethical breeders avoid over-breeding their female ball pythons. Female ball pythons should not be bred every season, as constant breeding can have adverse effects on their health. Give them ample time to recover between breeding cycles to ensure they remain healthy and stress-free.

4. Education and Awareness

Breeding should also be a way to educate others about the species. Sharing information about proper care, the importance of healthy breeding practices, and the significance of genetic diversity can help raise awareness and encourage others to follow ethical breeding standards.

UNDERSTANDING THE IMPACT ON THE BALL PYTHON POPULATION

Ball pythons are a popular species in the pet trade, and as a result, they have become one of the most bred reptiles in captivity. While breeding in captivity has helped to reduce the pressure on wild populations, it's crucial to consider how breeding practices can still impact the species in the long term.

1. Captive Breeding and Wild Populations

Ball pythons are native to Africa, and while their populations in the wild are currently stable, habitat destruction and illegal trade have posed threats to their numbers. By breeding ball pythons in captivity, breeders can contribute to reducing the demand for wild-caught specimens and help protect wild populations. However, it's essential to remain conscious of this broader ecological context.

2. Ensuring Sustainable Breeding Practices

Breeding should be done in a manner that is sustainable and doesn't contribute to the overproduction of snakes in the pet trade. Overproduction can lead to an oversupply in the market, making it harder for breeders to sell their hatchlings and, in turn, causing unhealthy practices such as culling or neglect. A responsible breeder focuses on breeding only what they can care for and sell, avoiding mass breeding that exceeds demand.

3. Preserving Genetic Diversity

Ethical breeders aim to maintain genetic diversity within their breeding programs to prevent genetic problems and inbreeding depression. The ball python gene pool can become limited over time, especially with rare morphs that are highly sought after. By introducing new genetic material into your breeding program, you help maintain a healthy and diverse population of ball pythons.

WORKING WITH REPUTABLE BREEDERS

As a breeder, it's important to work with reputable and ethical breeders who share your commitment to the health and well-being of the species. Building a network of responsible breeders helps ensure that you are part of a community that upholds high standards of care and breeding practices.

1. Research and Collaboration

Collaborating with reputable breeders can help you improve your breeding practices, exchange genetic material, and learn from the experiences of others. Make sure that the breeders you work with have a track record of healthy animals, responsible breeding practices, and a commitment to the species' welfare.

2. Avoiding Irresponsible Practices

Be mindful of breeders who engage in unethical practices, such as breeding snakes with known genetic defects, prioritizing profit over animal welfare, or producing animals for the sole purpose of catering to the demand for rare morphs. Aligning with breeders who share your ethical values will help promote a higher standard within the breeding community.

3. Transparency and Communication

Reputable breeders are transparent about their practices, the genetic backgrounds of their animals, and their breeding goals. They are willing to answer questions about the health and care of their snakes, and they provide full disclosure on the history and lineage of the animals they are selling.

LEGAL AND ETHICAL GUIDELINES IN BREEDING

Breeding ball pythons is subject to various legal and ethical guidelines that ensure the animals are treated with respect and that breeders follow established standards for animal care and commerce.

1. Complying with Local Laws and Regulations

Ensure that you are aware of and compliant with any local, state, or national laws regarding reptile breeding. In some regions, there may be specific licensing requirements or regulations surrounding the breeding and sale of exotic animals. Breeding without the proper permits or in violation of laws can lead to legal consequences and harm the reputation of responsible breeders.

2. Adhering to Animal Welfare Standards

It's important to adhere to animal welfare guidelines when breeding ball pythons. This includes providing suitable housing, appropriate temperature and humidity, proper nutrition, and a stress-free environment for your snakes. Neglecting these basic needs can result in health issues for the snakes and a poor reputation for the breeder.

3. Caring for Hatchlings and Ensuring Ethical Sales

Hatchlings must be raised in a responsible manner, with proper care and attention to their development. When selling hatchlings, ensure that buyers are knowledgeable about proper snake care and that they are prepared to meet the needs of the animals. Selling snakes to unprepared buyers or to those who will mistreat them is an unethical practice that can negatively impact the animals and your reputation as a breeder.

4. Ethical Selling and Pricing

Pricing should be fair and reflect the genetic quality and rarity of the morphs but should never be exorbitant or exploitative. Ethical pricing helps maintain the integrity of the breeding community and ensures that reptiles are accessible to those who can provide them with the proper care.

By approaching ball python breeding with ethical considerations in mind, breeders contribute to the long-term sustainability of the species, promote healthy practices within the breeding community, and ensure that these incredible reptiles are treated with respect and care. Ethical breeding isn't just about following the law—it's about fostering a culture of responsibility, education, and respect for the animals. Whether you are a hobbyist or a professional breeder, understanding and embracing these ethical principles will help you build a successful and responsible breeding program.

TROUBLESHOOTING AND COMMON MISTAKES

Breeding and caring for ball pythons can be an incredibly rewarding experience, but like any venture, it comes with its own set of challenges. Many new breeders and snake owners may encounter problems along the way, some of which could be avoided with the right knowledge and preparation. This chapter aims to help you troubleshoot common issues, avoid mistakes, and address unexpected behaviors, stress, illness, and other challenges that may arise.

COMMON BEGINNER MISTAKES AND HOW TO AVOID THEM

Starting with ball pythons can feel overwhelming, especially for first-time snake owners or breeders. Mistakes are part of the learning process, but it's essential to be aware of some common errors so you can avoid them.

1. Improper Enclosure Setup

One of the most common mistakes beginners make is not setting up the proper enclosure. This includes wrong temperature or humidity levels, improper substrate, and inadequate hides. Ball pythons need a secure and controlled environment to thrive. Make sure to use the correct substrate, ensure the temperature is in the right range (76-88°F, with a basking area of 90-92°F), and monitor humidity (50-60%) regularly.

2. Overfeeding or Underfeeding

Some beginners either overfeed or underfeed their ball pythons. Overfeeding can lead to obesity, while underfeeding may cause malnutrition. It's essential to follow a proper feeding schedule, offering appropriately sized prey and monitoring your snake's weight.

Generally, adult ball pythons can be fed every 7-14 days, while hatchlings may need food more frequently.

3. Inconsistent Handling

While ball pythons are typically calm, they require consistent handling to build trust and reduce stress. Handling too frequently or too roughly can make your snake anxious. Conversely, a lack of interaction may result in a shy or skittish snake. Start by gently handling your snake a few times a week, and gradually increase the frequency as the snake gets more accustomed to you.

4. Incorrect Lighting and Heating

Using the wrong type of heating source can be dangerous for your snake. Heat pads, ceramic heaters, or basking lamps are recommended, but be careful to avoid heating sources that can cause burns, such as hot rocks. A thermometer and hygrometer are essential tools to monitor the enclosure's temperature and humidity levels.

5. Mishandling Shedding

Improper shedding is a common problem. If your ball python is not shedding its skin correctly, it can cause serious health problems. Ensure your snake has enough humidity during the shedding process and provide a shedding box (a small container with damp sphagnum moss) to help your snake shed its skin properly. If stuck shed is left untreated, it can lead to retained eye caps or other skin issues.

HANDLING UNEXPECTED BALL PYTHON BEHAVIOR

Ball pythons are generally known for their calm and docile nature, but they can sometimes display unexpected behaviors. Understanding why these behaviors occur and how to respond can prevent unnecessary stress for both you and your snake.

1. Hiding or Being Reclusive

If your ball python is spending more time in its hide or seems to be reclusive, it's not necessarily a sign of illness. Ball pythons are nocturnal by nature and may prefer to stay hidden during the day. However, if your snake is consistently hiding and not eating, it could be a sign of stress, temperature issues, or even a health problem. Ensure that the enclosure's temperature and humidity are correct and that there are no environmental factors causing stress.

2. Striking or Defensive Behavior

Ball pythons are not naturally aggressive, but they may strike if they feel threatened or startled. If your snake is striking when you approach, give it some time to acclimate to its environment or to your presence. Be sure to handle your ball python gently and without sudden movements. If your snake is overly defensive, consider reducing handling time and ensuring that its enclosure is secure and stress-free.

3. Refusing Food

Refusing food is a common issue, especially during colder months when ball pythons may enter a natural period of dormancy or brumation. This can also happen if the snake is stressed, sick, or being offered the wrong type or size of prey. If your snake refuses food for more than a few weeks, consult a veterinarian to rule out underlying health issues.

4. Regurgitation of Food

Regurgitating food after eating is a sign of distress or illness. This can occur due to stress, overfeeding, or improper temperature and humidity. If your ball python regurgitates, allow it to rest for a few days without offering food, and ensure the enclosure is set up correctly. If the problem persists, seek veterinary advice.

DEALING WITH STRESS, ILLNESS, AND OTHER CHALLENGES

Stress and illness are common challenges faced by ball python breeders and owners. Being proactive in identifying and managing these issues is essential for the well-being of your snake.

1. Signs of Stress

Stress can manifest in many ways, including loss of appetite, erratic behavior, excessive hiding, or frequent shedding problems. Stress can be caused by environmental factors such as improper temperature, humidity, or handling. To reduce stress, maintain a consistent environment and avoid over-handling. Providing hides, ensuring the snake has enough space, and reducing loud noises in the room can also help.

2. Signs of Illness

Common signs of illness include lack of appetite, lethargy, difficulty shedding, wheezing or respiratory sounds, discharge from the nose or eyes, or abnormal feces. If your ball python shows any of these signs, it's essential to consult a reptile veterinarian as soon as possible for diagnosis and treatment.

3. Parasites and Infections

Parasites, including mites and worms, can affect ball pythons. If you notice tiny black spots on your snake's skin (mites), it may require a thorough cleaning of the enclosure and treatment with mite-specific medication. Internal parasites can lead to digestive issues, and fecal tests are essential for diagnosing these problems.

4. Brumation and Periods of Rest

Ball pythons may enter a state of brumation, which is similar to hibernation, during colder months. During this time, they may eat less or refuse food altogether. While it's normal for ball pythons to brumate, it's essential to ensure that the temperature and humidity levels remain consistent, and that the snake isn't stressed by the environmental change. If brumation seems prolonged or causes significant weight loss, consult a vet.

FREQUENTLY ASKED QUESTIONS

Q: How often should I handle my ball python?

A: Beginners should handle their ball python gently a few times per week for short periods. Gradually increase handling time as the snake becomes more accustomed to you. Avoid handling immediately after feeding, as it can cause stress and regurgitation.

Q: My ball python isn't eating. What should I do?

A: First, check the temperature and humidity in the enclosure. Ensure that the prey size is appropriate. If your snake still refuses food for more than a few weeks, it may be stressed, sick, or entering brumation. Consult a reptile vet if the issue persists.

Q: Can ball pythons live together in the same enclosure?

A: It's generally not recommended to house multiple ball pythons in the same enclosure due to the risk of stress, aggression, and competition for food. Male and female ball pythons should only be housed together during breeding season, and even then, supervision is necessary.

Q: How can I tell if my ball python is shedding properly?

A: During shedding, your ball python's skin will appear dull and its eyes will become blue and cloudy. Once the snake begins to shed, it will usually come off in one piece. If your snake has trouble shedding, increase humidity and provide a shedding box with moist moss. By understanding the common mistakes and how to troubleshoot issues, you can provide your ball python with the best possible care. Being proactive and attentive to your snake's needs will help ensure that it remains healthy, happy, and stress-free.

Conclusion

As we reach the end of this comprehensive guide, let's take a moment to recap the most important aspects of breeding and caring for ball pythons. Whether you're a first-time snake owner or an experienced breeder, the information provided in this book has been designed to give you the knowledge and tools necessary for a successful and rewarding experience with these fascinating creatures.

RECAP OF KEY BREEDING AND CARE TIPS

1. Choosing the Right Ball Python

The first step in your ball python journey is choosing a healthy, well-cared-for snake. Always select a snake from a reputable breeder or pet store, and make sure it shows no signs of illness or distress.

2. Creating the Perfect Habitat

Ball pythons require a well-maintained enclosure with the right temperature, humidity, and proper substrate. Providing them with secure hides and enrichment features will reduce stress and promote their well-being.

3. Feeding and Nutrition

Understanding your ball python's dietary needs is crucial. Offer appropriately sized prey, avoid overfeeding, and pay attention to feeding frequency. Ball pythons can be finicky eaters, so always check that the prey you're offering is suitable for your snake's age and size.

4. Handling and Socialization

Handle your snake gently and regularly to build trust, but avoid excessive handling that could cause stress. Allow your ball python time to acclimate to its new environment and always observe its behavior to ensure it feels comfortable.

5. Health Monitoring

Regularly check for signs of illness or stress. Knowing the symptoms of common diseases and conditions can help you act quickly and seek veterinary care if needed. Keep the enclosure clean and hygienic to prevent infections.

6. Breeding Considerations

When it comes to breeding, take the time to understand the reproductive cycle of ball pythons, and always ensure you have healthy breeding pairs. Breeding should never be rushed, and it's essential to have a clear plan in place for the care of hatchlings. Ethical considerations and responsible breeding practices should always be at the forefront of your decisions.

7. Advanced Breeding Techniques

As you gain experience, you'll have the opportunity to experiment with selective breeding and explore the exciting world of morphs. However, always remember to track genetics carefully and work with reputable breeders to maintain the health of the ball python population.

8. Troubleshooting and Problem-Solving

Throughout your journey, you may face challenges such as feeding issues, stress, illness, or breeding difficulties. Address these challenges with patience and seek help from experienced breeders or veterinarians when needed. By remaining calm and informed, you'll be well-equipped to handle any problems that arise.

9. Ethical Breeding Practices

Always prioritize the well-being of your ball pythons. Ethical breeding practices involve breeding for the right reasons, minimizing the impact on the overall ball python population, and following legal and ethical guidelines to ensure that the snakes you produce are healthy and well cared for.

NEXT STEPS IN YOUR BALL PYTHON JOURNEY

Now that you have a thorough understanding of ball python care and breeding, your next steps will depend on where you are in your journey:

1. Get Hands-On Experience

If you're new to keeping ball pythons, start by setting up your enclosure and getting to know your snake. Practice regular handling, and observe its behavior to learn how to care for it properly. If you've already started breeding, continue refining your breeding practices and keep detailed records of each pairing.

2. Expand Your Knowledge

Stay informed about new trends in the ball python community. Join online forums, attend reptile expos, and network with other breeders to continue learning. The world of morphs, genetics, and breeding strategies is ever-evolving, so there's always something new to discover.

3. Focus on Breeding Ethics

If you're planning to breed your ball pythons, consider your goals carefully. Ensure that you're breeding responsibly, with an emphasis on producing healthy offspring and contributing positively to the hobby. Ethical breeding practices are crucial to ensuring the future of ball pythons in captivity.

4. Invest in Your Breeding Program

For those aiming to build a successful breeding program, start investing in quality breeding pairs, track genetic information carefully, and research the various morphs and their genetic traits. Consider how you'll market and sell your hatchlings and ensure that you're complying with all legal and ethical guidelines.

5. Veterinary Care and Continued Health Monitoring

Always prioritize regular veterinary checkups for your ball pythons. Preventative care, including parasite control and early detection of illnesses, can help ensure that your snakes remain healthy for years to come.

6. Be Patient and Enjoy the Journey

Whether you're new to ball pythons or you've been breeding them for years, remember that patience is key. Every snake has its own personality, and breeding requires time and care. Enjoy the process of learning and growing with your ball pythons, and take pride in the healthy, thriving snakes you raise. Your journey with ball pythons is a continuous learning experience. The knowledge gained from this guide will help you make informed decisions as you care for and breed these incredible snakes. Stay dedicated, stay curious, and most importantly, enjoy the fascinating world of ball pythons!

www.ingramcontent.com/pod-product-compliance
Lightning Source LLC
Chambersburg PA
CBHW072245260726
48659CB00004BA/1359

9 798302 092748